Name _____

Bones

Fish, birds, frogs, cats, and snakes are like you in one important way. They all have bones. These bones help the fish to swim. They help the bird to fly. Bones help the cat to run and climb. They help the frog to hop and the snake to slither. Bones help you and me to run, jump, and to stand up.

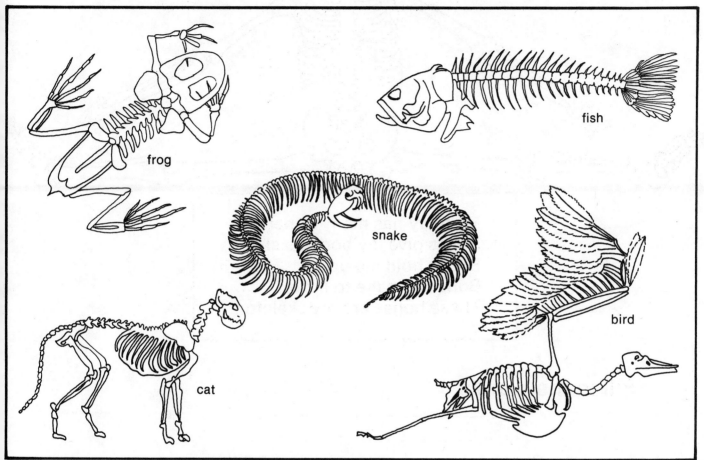

Answer the questions:

1. How are you like a fish, frog, or snake?

_____

_____

_____

2. How do bones help you?

_____

_____

_____

Extra: Draw another animal that has bones on the back of this paper.

Name _____

My Skeleton

> My body has many bones.
> Bones give my body its shape.
> Bones hold me up.
> Bones help me to move.
> These bones are my skeleton.

Fill in the blanks:

_____

1. Bones _____ me up.

2. Bones give my body _____.

3. Bones help me to _____.

4. These bones are called a _____.

Extra: Turn this paper over. Draw what you would look like if you didn't have any bones.

Name _____

Bones Have Many Uses

Some bones in my skeleton have special jobs.
These bones protect the soft parts of my body.

The bones in the top of my
skull protect my brain.

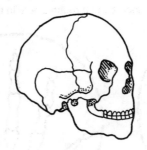

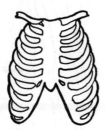

The bones in my ribcage
protect my heart and
lungs.

The bones in my backbone
protect the nerves inside.

Many bones have red marrow inside. The red marrow makes new blood
for my body.

Some bones in my skeleton store minerals that help my body work.

Match:

1. Bones in the skull   the nerves inside.

2. The ribcage protects   protect your brain.

3. The backbone protects   your heart and lungs.

4. Some bones store   make new blood.

5. The inside of some bones   minerals.

Extra: Circle the words on this page that name bones.

The Dancing Skeleton

1. Cut out all the pieces on pages 4, 5 and 6.
2. Paste the heart and lungs on to the chest piece. (Put paste only where marked.)
3. Paste the ribs over the lungs.
4. Paste the skull piece over the brain. (Put paste only on the flap portion.)
5. Connect all pieces with brass paper fasteners.
6. Loop a rubberband through a hole in the skull.

4

MY SKELETONS AND MUSCLES

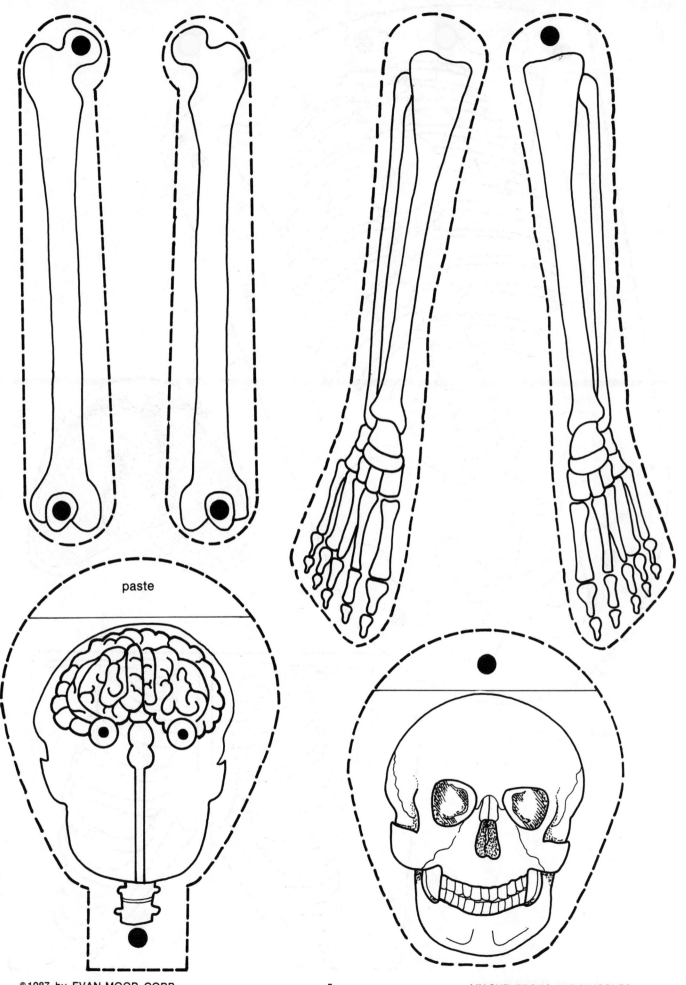

paste

5

MY SKELETONS AND MUSCLES

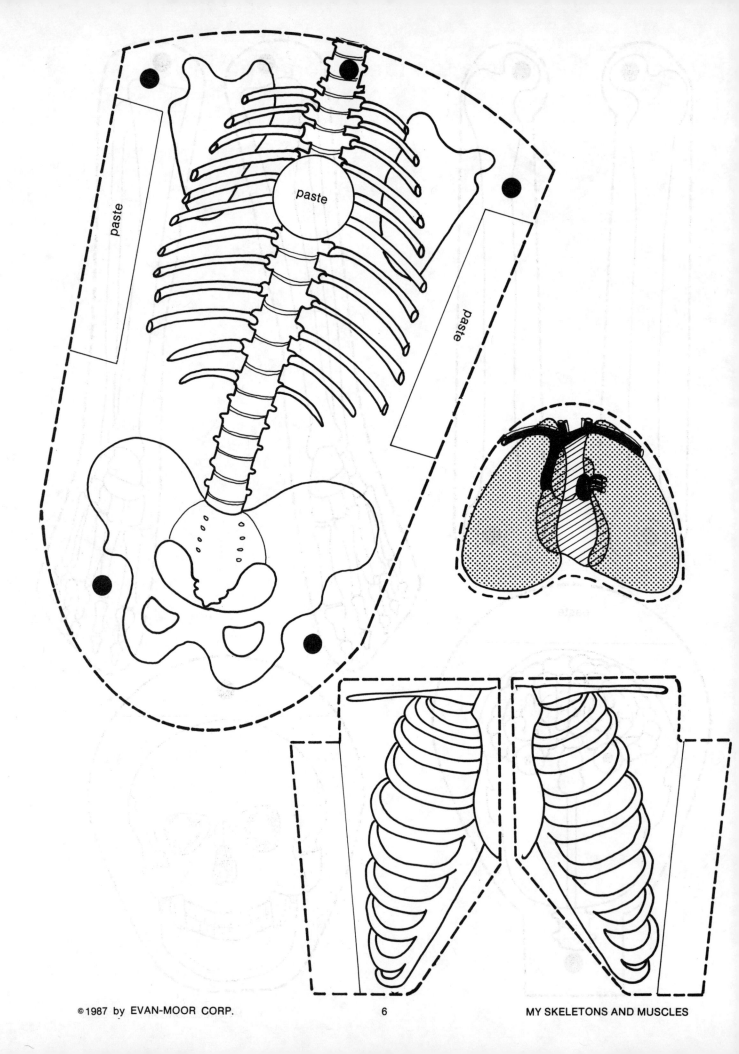

paste

paste

paste

Where do these bones go?

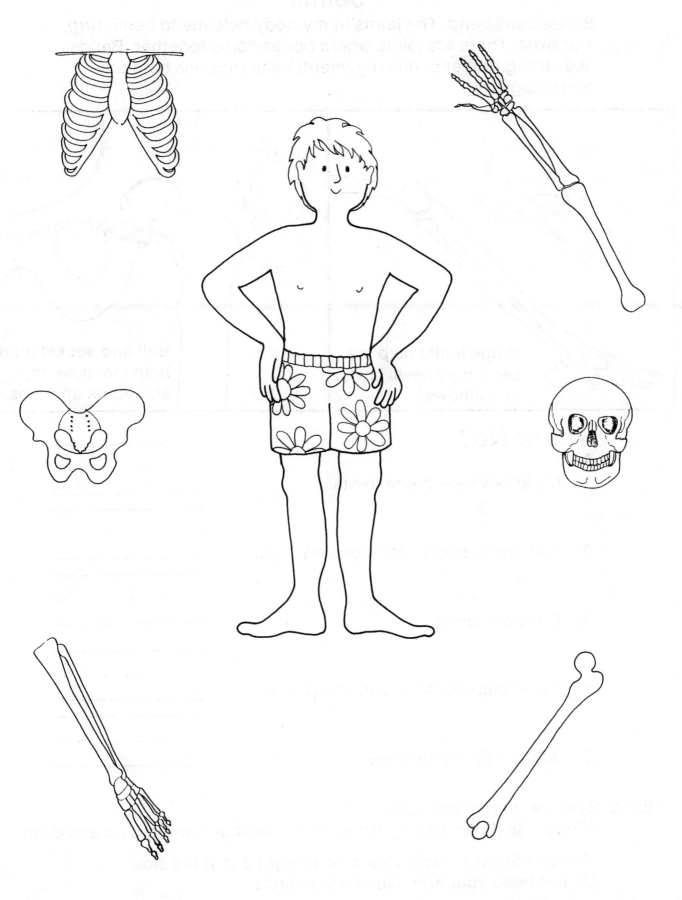

Name _____

Joints

Bones can't bend. The joints in my body help me to bend, turn, and twist. There are joints where bones come together. Bands like strong rubber bands (ligaments) and muscles hold the bones together.

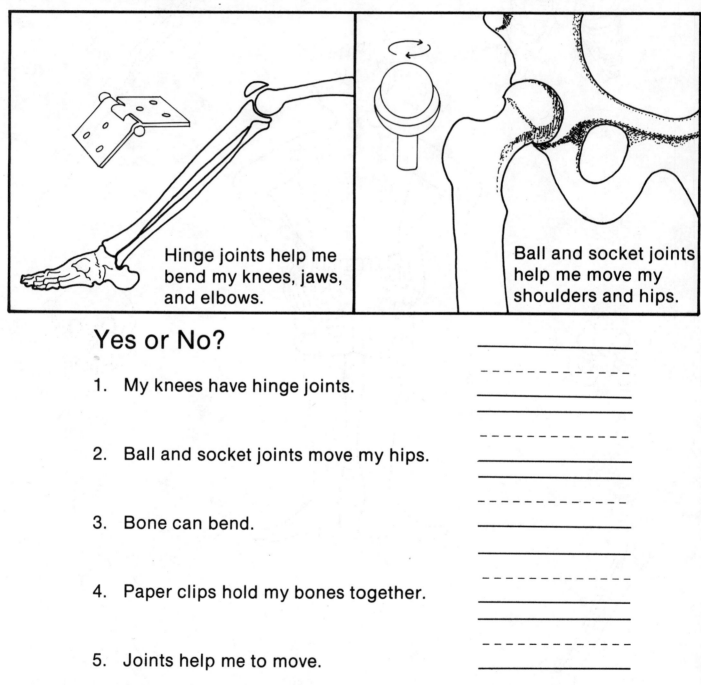

Hinge joints help me bend my knees, jaws, and elbows.

Ball and socket joints help me move my shoulders and hips.

Yes or No?

1. My knees have hinge joints.

2. Ball and socket joints move my hips.

3. Bone can bend.

4. Paper clips hold my bones together.

5. Joints help me to move.

Extra: See how your joints work.

Hinge - Sit down. Bend your knee. Move your lower leg up and down.

Ball and Socket - Hold your arm straight out at the side. Do not bend your arm. Move it in a circle.

8   MY SKELETONS AND MUSCLES

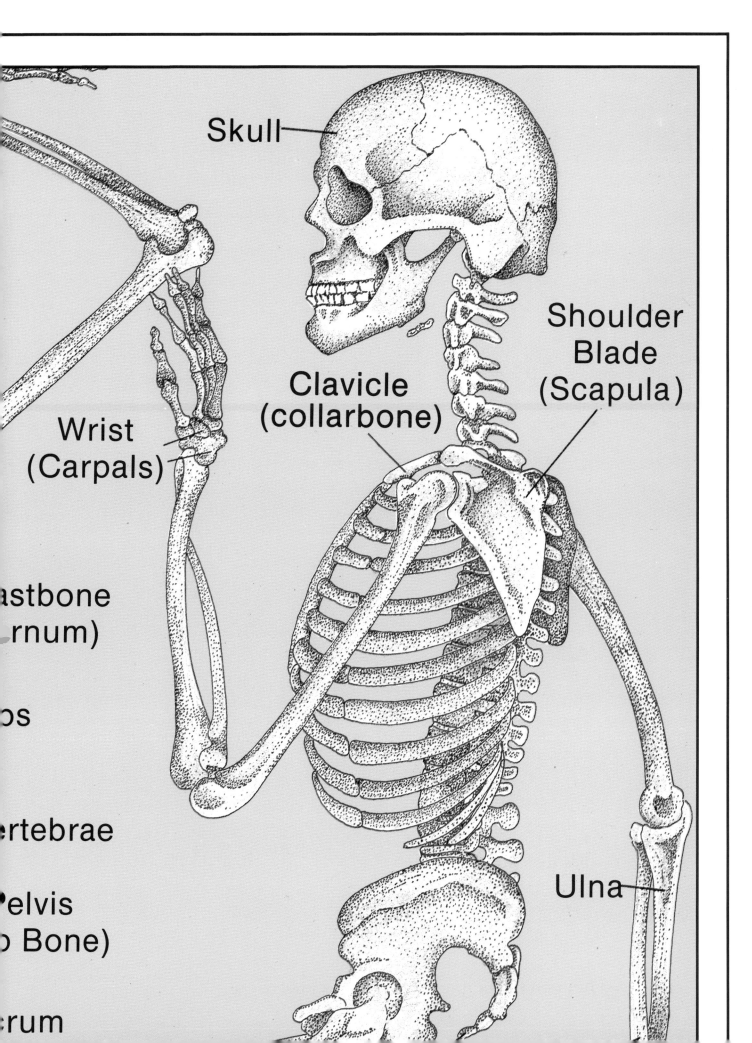

Skull

Shoulder
Blade
(Scapula)

Clavicle
(collarbone)

Wrist
(Carpals)

astbone
rnum)

os

ertebrae

Pelvis
Bone)

Ulna

crum

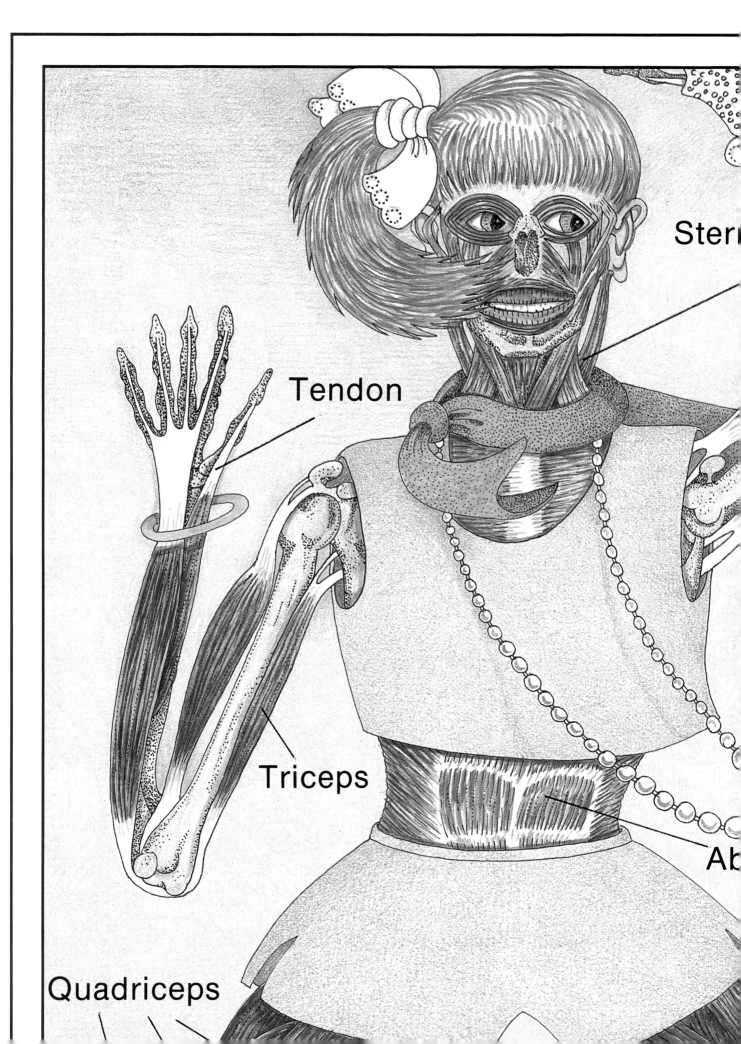

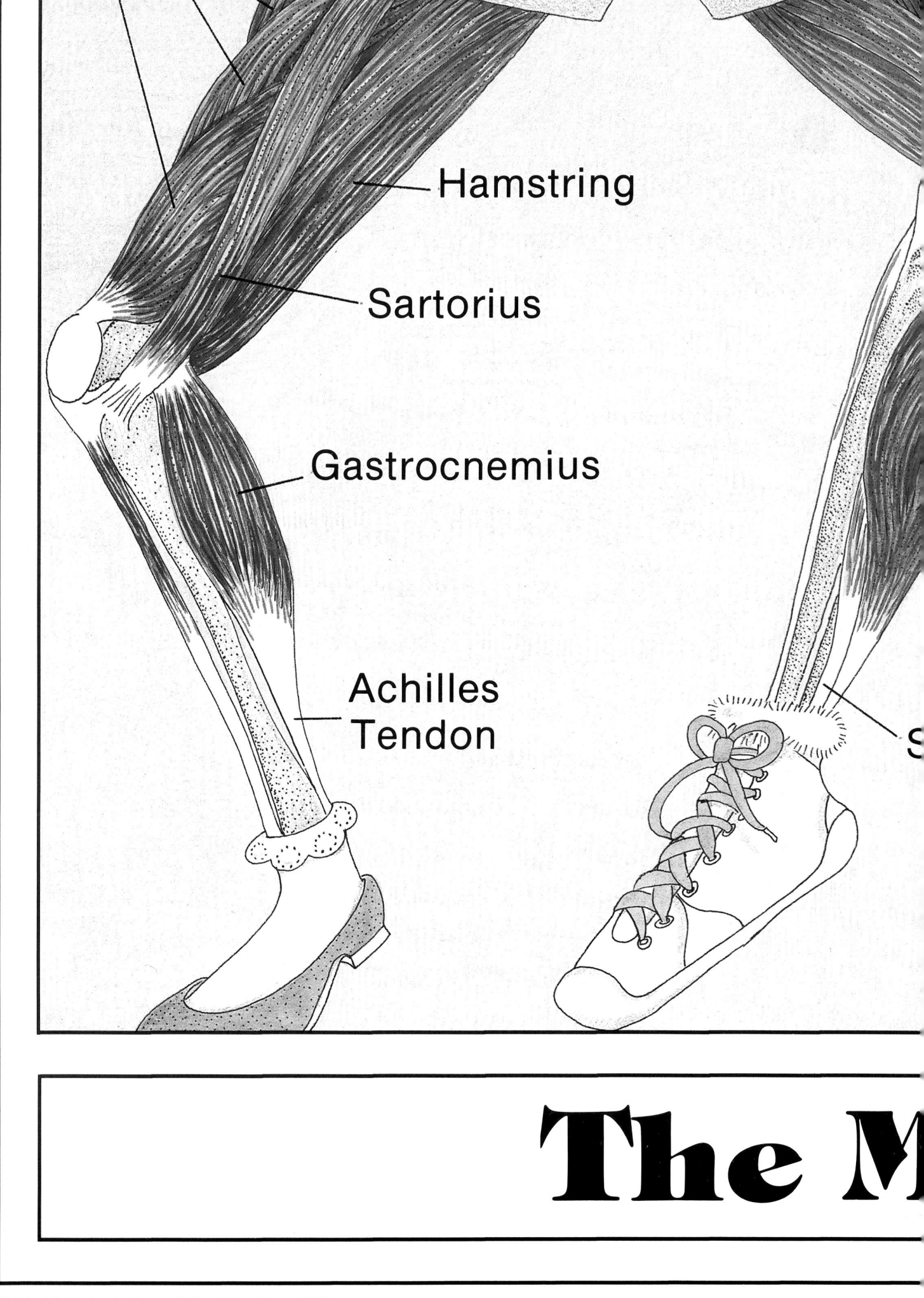

Hamstring

Sartorius

Gastrocnemius

Achilles
Tendon

The M

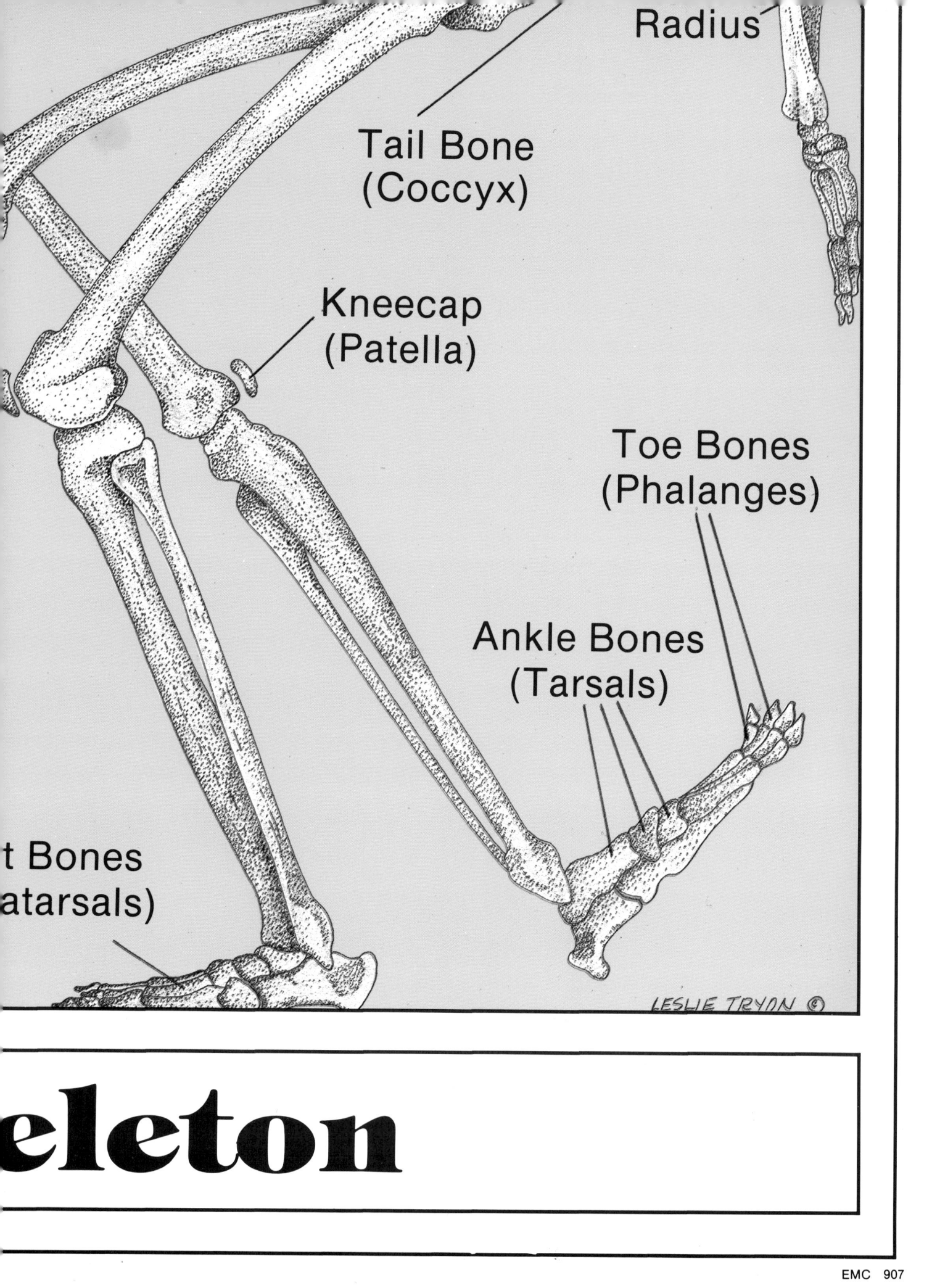

Radius

Tail Bone
(Coccyx)

Kneecap
(Patella)

Toe Bones
(Phalanges)

Ankle Bones
(Tarsals)

t Bones
atarsals)

LESLIE TRYON ©

eleton

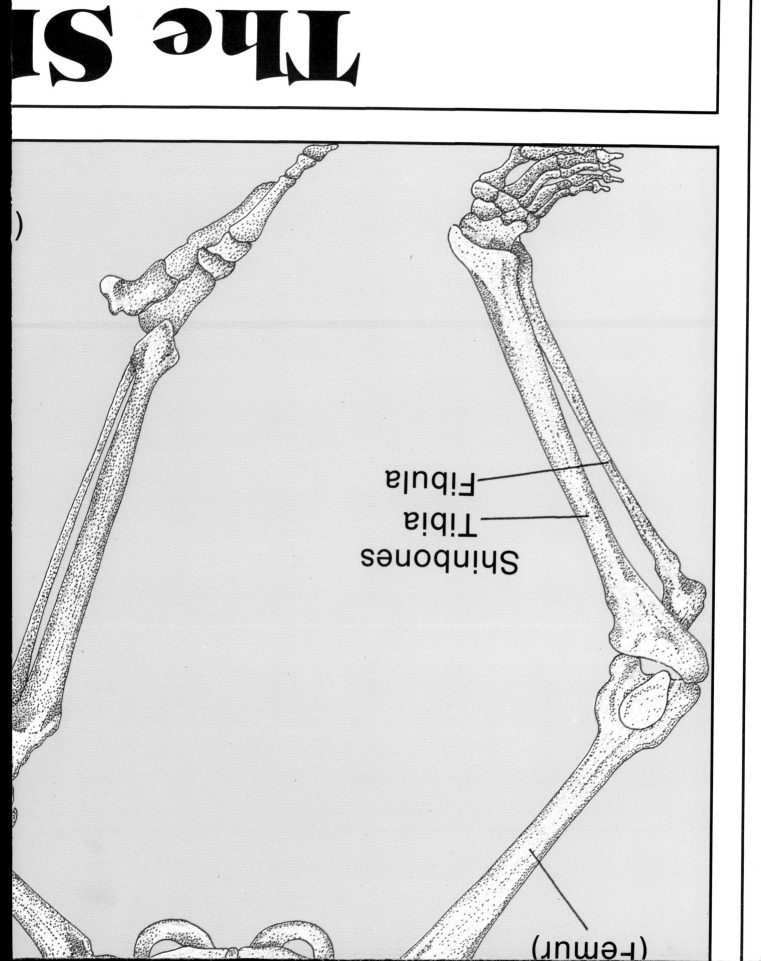

The S

(Femur)

Shinbones
Tibia
Fibula

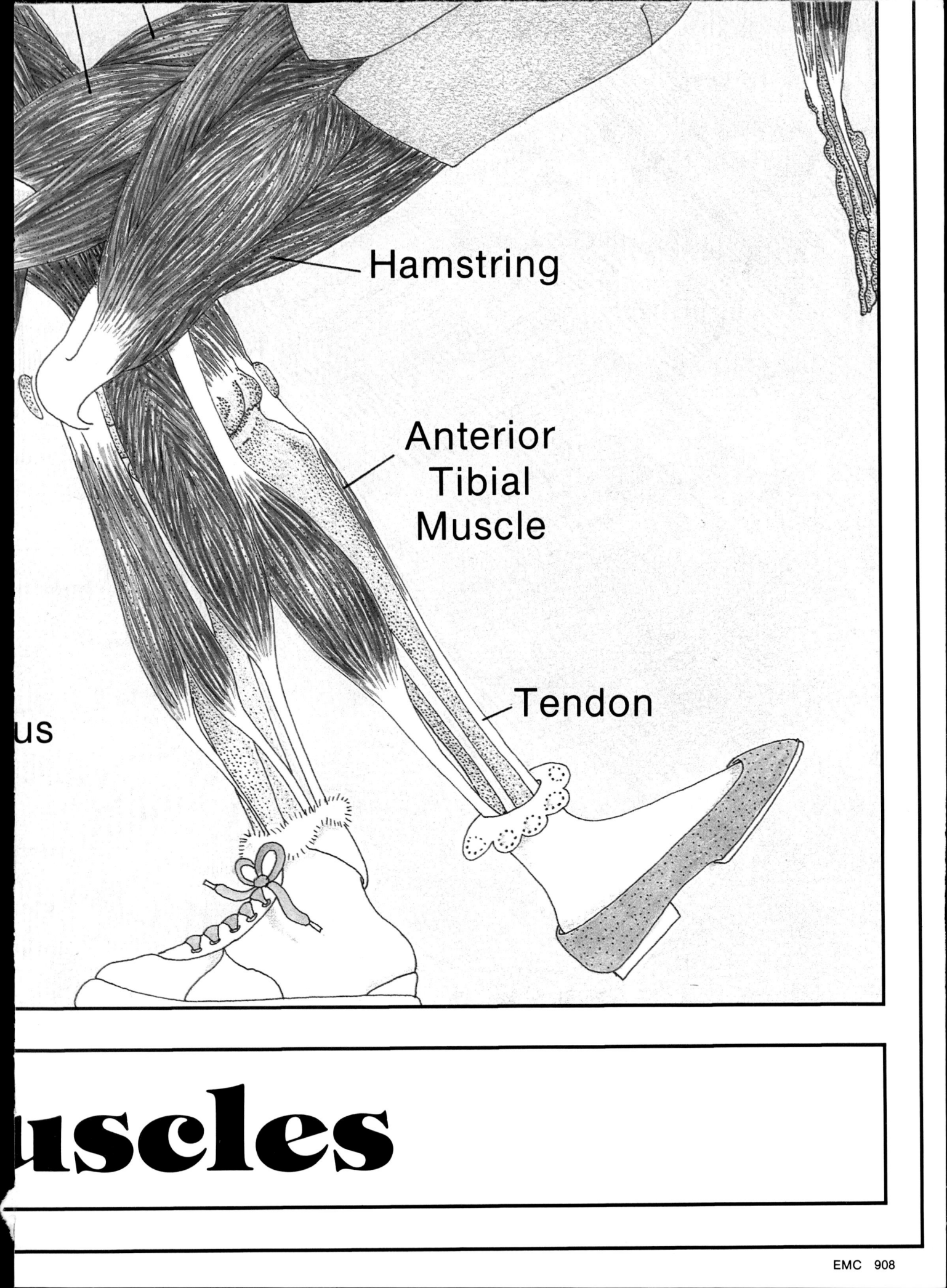

Hamstring

Anterior
Tibial
Muscle

Tendon

us

uscles

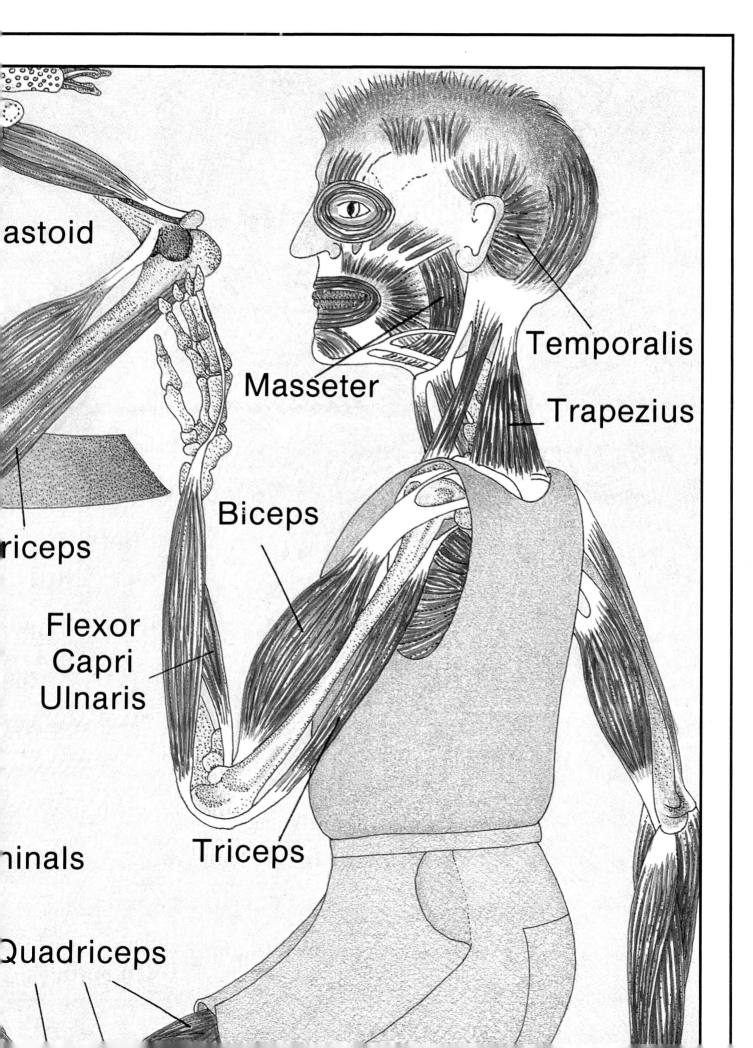

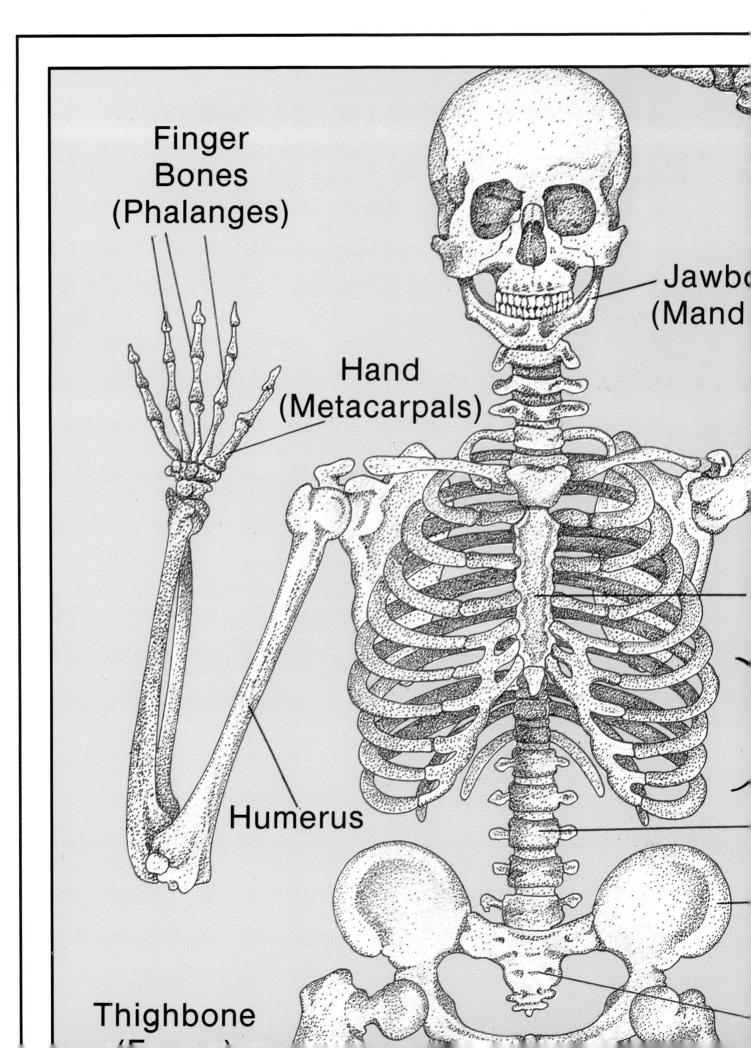

Finger
Bones
(Phalanges)

Hand
(Metacarpals)

Jawbo
(Mand

Humerus

Thighbone

Name _____

Broken Bones

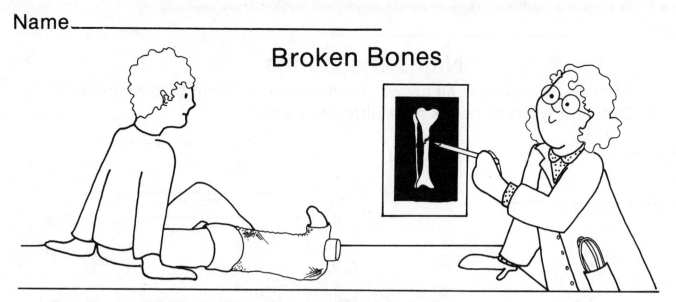

Bones can break if they are bent too far.
A doctor will take an x-ray to see where the break is.
The doctor will fit the broken bone back together. A cast is put on to keep the bone from moving while it is getting well. After many weeks the cast can come off and you can run and play again.

Ask 20 people "Have you ever broken a bone?"

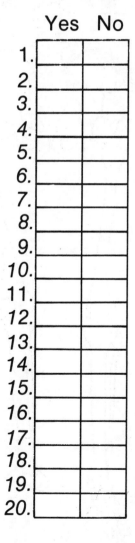

	Yes	No
1.		
2.		
3.		
4.		
5.		
6.		
7.		
8.		
9.		
10.		
11.		
12.		
13.		
14.		
15.		
16.		
17.		
18.		
19.		
20.		

Name _____

Name the Bones

After my bones have all grown, I will have a skeleton of 206 bones. Different types of bones have different names.

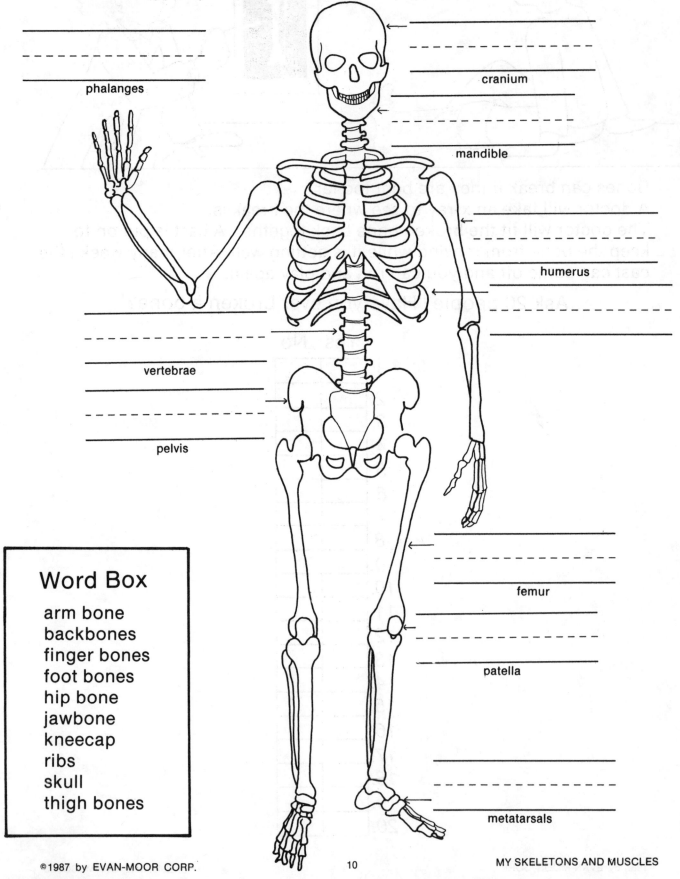

phalanges

cranium

mandible

humerus

vertebrae

pelvis

femur

patella

metatarsals

Word Box

arm bone
backbones
finger bones
foot bones
hip bone
jawbone
kneecap
ribs
skull
thigh bones

10

MY SKELETONS AND MUSCLES

Name _____

My Muscles

I have more than 600 muscles.

Each muscle has a job to do.

Without muscles I could not run or play.

Muscles help me wink, smile, bend,
and kick a ball.

Muscles move the bones in my skeleton.
Muscles move food and blood around my body.
Muscles help my lungs to breathe and my heart to beat.
When any part of my body moves, my muscles are working.

Yes or no?

1. Muscles are at work when my body moves.

   - - - - - - - - - - - -

2. Bones move the food and blood in my body.

   - - - - - - - - - - - -

3. I need muscles to help me breathe.

   - - - - - - - - - - - -

4. I have over 900 muscles.

   - - - - - - - - - - - -

5. I have muscles that help me smile.

   - - - - - - - - - - - -

Extra: Color the muscles in the picture.

Name _____

More About Muscles

Strong bands (tendons) hold the muscles to my bones. Nerves in the muscles take messages to my brain. These messages tell the muscles when to move and when to rest.

> Color the bones yellow.
> Color the muscles red.
> Color the tendons blue.

> **Write these words on the lines:**
> bones   tendons   muscles

Extra: Look at the tendons in the back of your hand.
Wiggle your fingers to see them move.
Feel the large tendon at the back of your ankle.

Name _____

How Muscles Work

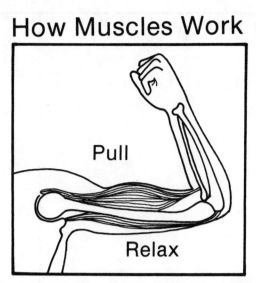

Pull

Relax

Muscles cannot push. They can only pull. When a muscle gets shorter, it pulls the bone or body part to a new position. When the muscle relaxes, the bone or body part goes back to its first position.

I can keep my muscles strong by getting healthy exercise.

Put an X on the muscles that are pulling.
Put a ✓ on the muscles that are relaxed.

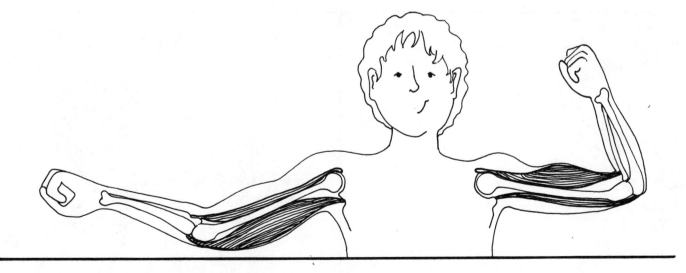

Extra: Color the bones in each picture.

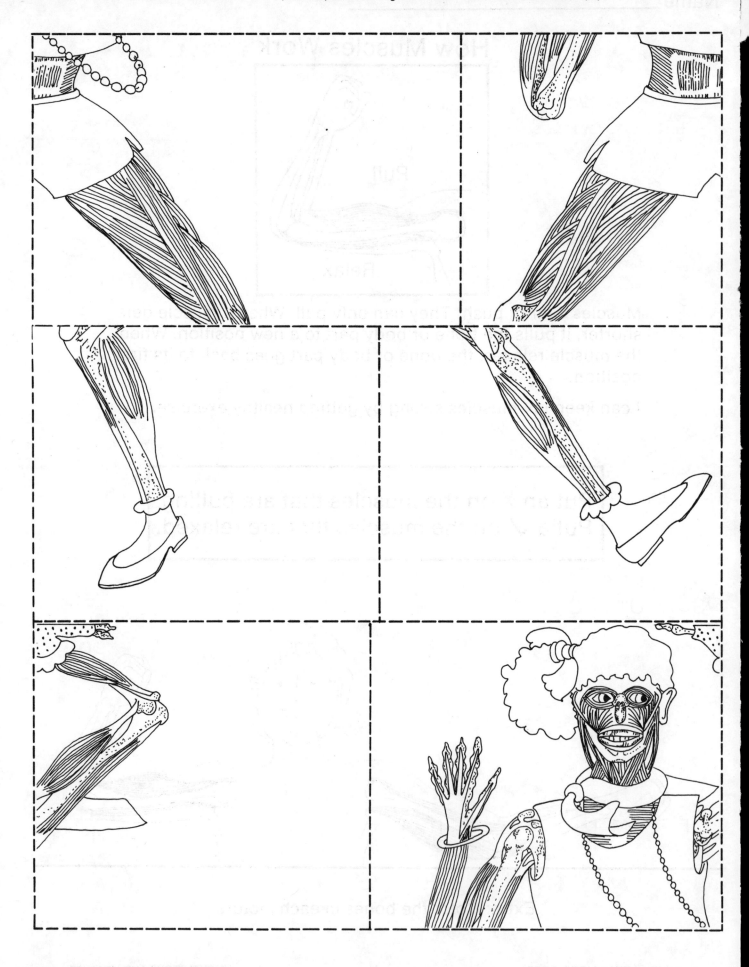

MY SKELETONS AND MUSCLES

Name_____

WHAT AM I?

1. I am the bone that helps protect your brain.

_____

- - - - - - - - - - - -

_____

2. We are the bones that protect your heart and lungs.

- - - - - - - - - - - -

_____

3. I am the bone that moves when you chew.

_____

- - - - - - - - - - - -

_____

4. We are the bones you use when you pick up something.

_____

- - - - - - - - - - - -

_____

5. I am the long bone in your leg.

_____

- - - - - - - - - - - -

_____

6. We help your bones to move.

_____

- - - - - - - - - - - -

_____

ribs
(ribcage)

fingerbones
(phalanges)

jawbone
(mandible)

thigh bone
(femur)

skull
(cranium)

muscles

WORD SEARCH

```
R K N E E C A P T H S
I J O I N T S B E I K
B S K E L E T O N P U
S M U S C L E N D B L
X J A W B O N E O O L
B O N E B O N E N N Z
F I N G E R B O N E S
```

FINGER BONES   MUSCLE
HIP BONE   RIBS
JAWBONE   SKELETON
JOINTS   SKULL
KNEECAP   TENDON

Find BONE and circle it with green.
I found bone_____times in the word search.

Extra:

```
C P H U M E R U S P
F E M U R T I B I A
U L C R A N I U M T
L V E R T E B R A E
N I C O C C Y X Z L
A S R I B C A G E L
M A N D I B L E X A
```

CRANIUM   PATELLA
COCCYX   PELVIS
FEMUR   RIBCAGE
HUMERUS   TIBIA
MANDIBLE   ULNA
           VERTEBRAE

Teacher: Run 8 copies of this page on tagboard (or paste to thin cardboard). Laminate or cover the pages with clear
          Contact and cut the cards apart. Children play the game like "Go Fish". Example: "Do you have Skeleton #1?"
          "No. Go Fish." The first person to complete the whole skeleton wins.

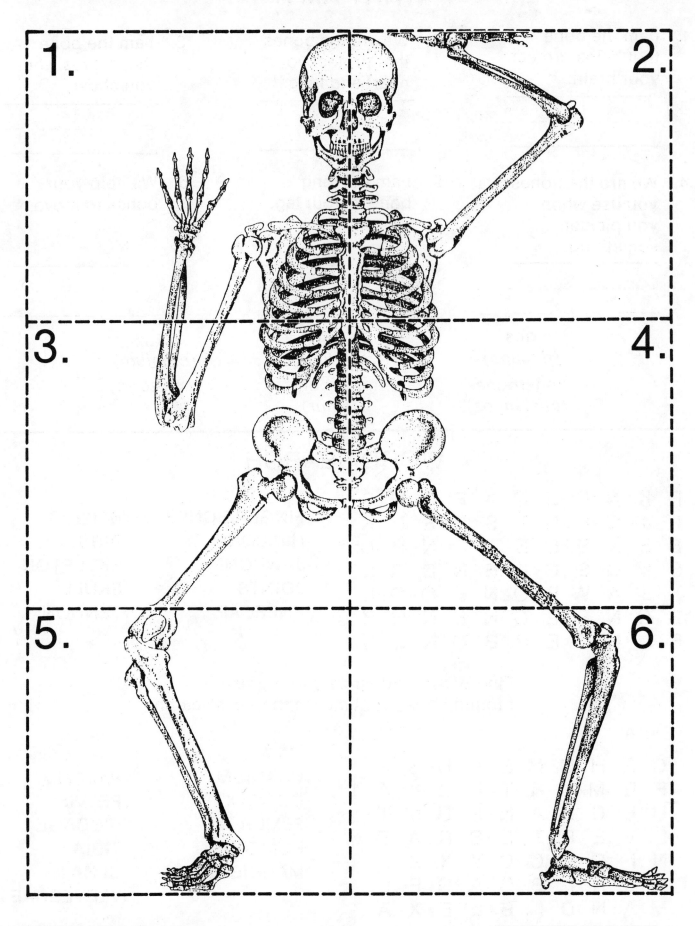